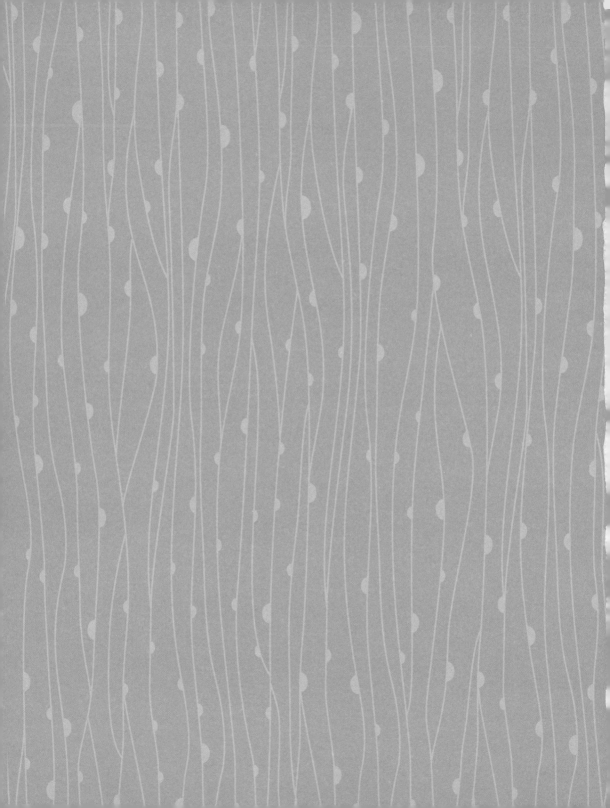

Wit & Wisdom
from the
GARDEN

ISBN-13: 978-1-60433-716-7
ISBN-10: 1-60433-716-8

This book may be ordered by mail from the publisher. Please include $5.99 for postage and handling.
Please support your local bookseller first!

Books published by Cider Mill Press Book Publishers are available at special discounts for bulk purchases
in the United States by corporations, institutions, and other organizations. For more information,
please contact the publisher.

Cider Mill Press Book Publishers
"Where good books are ready for press"
PO Box 454
12 Spring Street
Kennebunkport, Maine 04046

Visit us on the Web!
www.cidermillpress.com

Cover design by Kali Potito and Alicia Freile, Tango Media
Interior design by Mark Voss Design
Layout by Alicia Freile, Tango Media
Typography: Chalkduster, Hmk Handsome AC, Hmk Handyman Condensed, Minion Pro,
and Trade Gothic
All images used under official license from Shutterstock.com.

Printed in China

1 2 3 4 5 6 7 8 9 0
First Edition

Wit & Wisdom
from the
GARDEN

Over 75 Gardening and Canning
Tips, Plus Recipes for Enjoying
Your Bountiful Harvest

by Emily Mills

CIDER MILL
PRESS

BOOK
PUBLISHERS

Kennebunkport, ME

For Mom, Dad, Joshua, and Grandma.
May our roots always be planted in each other's love.

ON
GARDENING

Square One

Plotting your garden and digging up the grass can be difficult and stressful. Take the trouble out of it by layering cardboard on top of your grass in the desired shape and size. Then, cover with mulch or compost (about 6 inches). Keep the area moist until it's compacted, and after a month or two you should have the perfect bed to plant in.

Blown Away?

If you live in a windy area, make sure to plant tougher shrubs in the path of the gusts. They'll protect your smaller, more delicate flowers and crops.

"A FLOWER BLOSSOMS FOR ITS OWN JOY."

Oscar Wilde

COLOR YOUR GARDEN!

Indulge in a lesson on color: complementary colors create a very different scheme than analogous ones. Pairing colors that are opposite from one another on the color wheel such as blue and orange or yellow and purple create an exciting, bold statement. By contrast, pairing colors in the same family such as pink, purple, and blue creates a softer pattern.

Keeping Flowers Vibrant

Looking to maximize your flowers' full, vibrant potential? Pay attention to heat and light sensitivity as well as the soil's acidity. Plants can also experience stress, especially after being transplanted. Stress may cause flowers to fade, but don't worry, they should regain their color in no time!

Container Gardening

If you're pressed for space, don't let that deter you from trying out your green thumb. Container gardening allows you to grow anywhere with enough light! You won't have to worry about weeding and you can bring your plants inside at night to protect from frost and critters!

Container gardens also allow you to get creative! Think about repurposing household items to create decorative containers — anything from rain boots to old crates!

INSTANT SUCCESS: STRAWBERRIES

Strawberries grow like weeds, and there are many ways to get them started! Keep them in pots or plant them in an apple barrel so that you can control them as they grow. You won't believe how much sweeter homegrown berries are than store-bought ones!

Mulching your garden has many benefits! Mulch kills the weeds that steal nutrients from your plants and also helps keep moisture in the soil. There are many types of mulch available, some that are organic and some that are made of other materials, such as plastic!

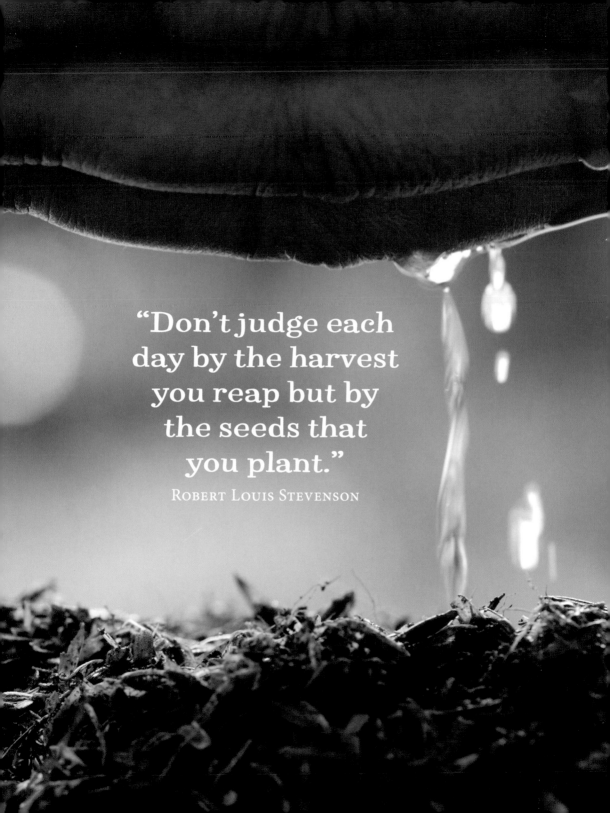

"Don't judge each day by the harvest you reap but by the seeds that you plant."

ROBERT LOUIS STEVENSON

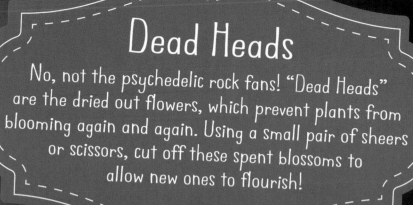

Dead Heads

No, not the psychedelic rock fans! "Dead Heads" are the dried out flowers, which prevent plants from blooming again and again. Using a small pair of sheers or scissors, cut off these spent blossoms to allow new ones to flourish!

Looking to bring nature's music into your garden? Refrain from "dead heading" certain flowers like bee balm, aster, columbine, and zinnia. Songbirds such as finches, sparrows, and cardinals find the seeds of these flowers very attractive and will come to feed and sing!

PERSISTENCE IS EVERYTHING

Gardening doesn't always go as planned. Planting something new can bring obstacles and challenges you did not foresee, but be persistent. Keep your head high and try again next season!

SHINE A LITTLE LIGHT

Plant your crops in order of shortest
to tallest. Paying close attention to
the direction of the sun, make sure
the tall crops never overshadow
the shorter ones.

I'm A Beginner–
What Should I Plant?

If you're just starting out, try planting
these crops. They're easy to care
for and fruitful (in other words,
a nice confidence booster)!

- Tomatoes
- Lettuce
- Cucumbers
- Squash
- Radishes
- Sunflowers
- Beans
- Peas
- Rhubarb

"EVERY FLOWER IS A SOUL BLOSSOMING IN NATURE."

GERARD DE NERVAL

Gardening may take time but it rewards those who dont make hasty mistakes!

Pressure Treated Wood

When you're building garden beds, trellises, etc. never use pressure treated wood. The chemicals used in it can be very toxic to the soil, plants, and to you. Instead try cedar, oak, or spruce!

COMPOSTING: THE BASICS

Composting yields amazing nutrient-rich humus. It's all about layering and balance. You want to maintain equal parts of nitrogen and carbon. What does this mean? In a very basic sense, carbon tends to be "brown," such as pine needles and leaves. Nitrogen tends to be "green," such as grass clippings, flowers, and fruits/vegetables. Once you've built your compost pile it'll do a lot of the work by itself. You can give it a boost by mixing it, adding manure, and making sure it is always damp. Let rainwater keep it moist, or if you're in a drier region, water periodically (but don't soak it)!

DIY Compost Bin

Compost bins are very easy to make in just an
afternoon. All you need are a handful of wooden pallets
(make sure the wood is not treated), deck screws, and
a drill. Screw together the pallets, leaving the bottom
and one side open. If you want to keep critters out,
you may also want to screw on a top and a hinged
door to your bin. Alternatively, you can use
chicken wire or fencing to create
a similar structure.

Watering Time!

The best time to water your garden is the early morning, allowing the sun to have plenty of time to dry the morning dew off the leaves of your plants. If you water at dusk, the droplets may remain on the leaves, which gives mold the opportunity to grow. Keep in mind that however you choose to water, make sure it isn't too forceful! You don't ever want to wash away soil from your plants as this protects them and feeds them nutrients.

"If you have a garden and a library, you have everything you need."

CICERO

DRIP IRRIGATION AND SOAKER HOSES

Consider installing drip irrigation or soaker hoses in your garden—both are relatively inexpensive, allow you to target certain plants, and reduce wasted water. It's best to install these systems in the early spring to avoid crushing your plants!

DIY Drip Irrigation

If your garden is smaller and you don't want to invest in soaker hoses or drip irrigation, you can create your own! Next to each plant, bury a milk jug or soda bottle that you have punctured holes in. Simply refill it with water whenever the soil feels dry!

REUSE, REUSE, REUSE!

Once you've had your cup of morning coffee, save your grounds to add to your garden and/or compost pile. Not only do they provide nutrients to your plants but they also deter insects.

Crack Down On Pests!

Eggshells can be a beneficial addition to both your garden and your compost pile. Rinse them off, crush them, and then simply spread around the base of your plants. You'll have a natural insect repellent and a great source of calcium, too!

Got Weeds?

Need an easy, inexpensive, *and* nontoxic solution to problematic weeds? Vinegar! All you have to do is mix regular white vinegar with one teaspoon of dish soap into a spray bottle and you're ready to battle the weeds! Use on a warm, sunny day and be careful not to get too close to your plants.

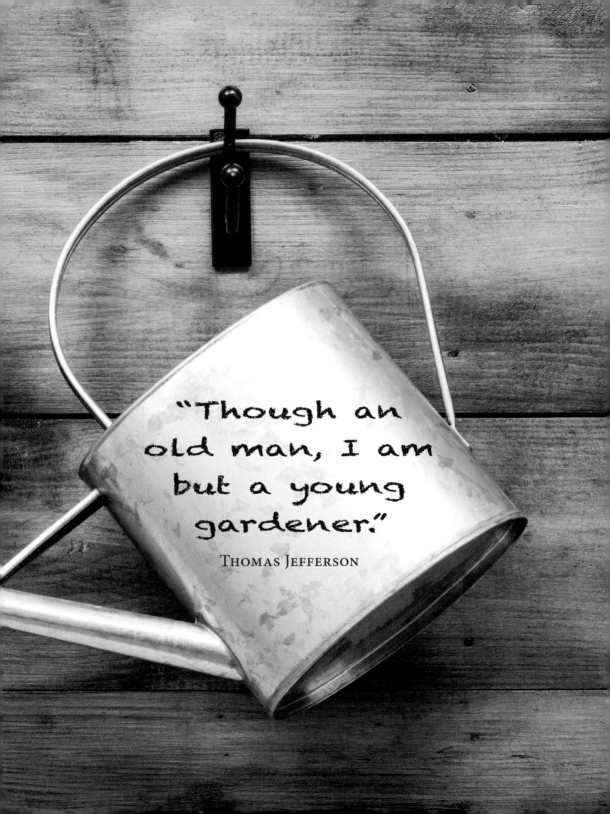

The Drunken Slug

Slugs are not only unsightly but can also damage
the plants in your garden. Leave a dish of beer out
in your garden—it attracts and kills slugs
leaving your garden slime-free.

Critter Control: L-shaped fencing

One of the most frustrating parts of gardening is discovering a critter has gotten to your fruits and vegetables. Groundhogs are the culprits time and time again. Dig a trench at least six inches deep and at least six inches wide. Bury your fence in this trench in an "L" shape so that no matter what direction the groundhog digs, it will only reach fence!

DIY HOOP HOUSE

Hoop houses are easy, multifunctional gardening tools. They can protect your plants from weather and critters, all the while helping control the climate in your garden. All you need is ½ or ¾ inch-diameter flexible plastic tubing, 18-22 inch stakes, wooden beams or bricks for weight, garden clips, and whatever material you plan to use on top. Plastic, for example, can be used to create a green house. Netting, on the other hand, protects your plants from unwanted birds, bugs, and creatures. Create arches by bending the tubing and inserting the stakes into each end. Then drape your choice of plastic or fabric over the tubing, attaching it to the stakes with the clips. Finally, weigh down the sides with wood or bricks.

Natural Fungicide

Mushrooms can steal valuable nutrients from the plants in your garden as they grow. Keep them out of your garden by sprinkling a teaspoon or two of cinnamon around each one!

DIY Seed Sower

Want to save money and time when planting your seeds? Take wine corks and push them onto the prongs of a garden rake. Now you'll be able to create drills—the shallow seeding holes you typically make with a small shovel or your fingers. Just drop your seeds in after creating rows!

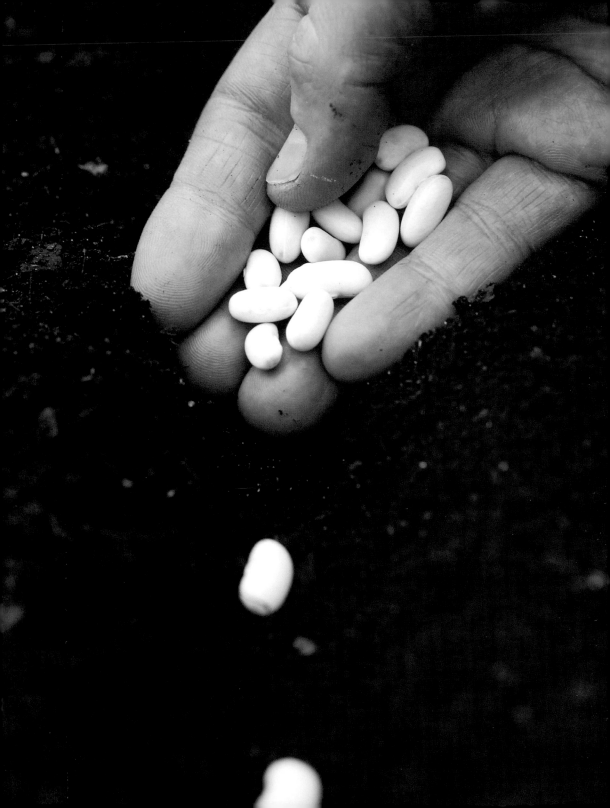

DIY Seed Spacing Sticks

Many seeds need to be carefully spaced a certain distance apart. Simply take a long stick and mark it with the distance your seeds require—typically around 2 inches. Hammer or drill nails in at each of these marks. Once you've created this tool, there is no guesswork. Just lay the stick down and you'll know exactly where to place your seeds.

"I HAD RATHER BE ON MY FARM THAN BE EMPEROR OF THE WORLD."

GEORGE WASHINGTON

AVOCADO TREE

Avocados have been getting quite a bit of attention lately because they are super foods that are absolutely delicious! Want to try growing your own? All you need is an avocado pit, three toothpicks, a cup, and some water.

1. Find the hilum of your avocado pit. This is the round part on the top of the pit and is where the tree will begin to grow from. It is opposite of the slightly pointed part of the pit.

2. Place the hilum face down and insert the three toothpicks equidistant from each other about ¼ of an inch into the side of the pit.

3. Suspend the pit by the toothpicks on the edge of the cup and fill the cup with enough water to cover the hilum.

4. Place in a sunny window and wait for roots to grow.

5. Once you see roots forming, you can add soil to your cup to provide nutrients.

6. When it has outgrown its cup, plant the baby trees into a larger pot that it'll grow into!

Jot It Down!

One of my favorite ways to learn about your success and shortfalls from season to season is keeping a garden journal. Use your journal to record what you planted, their growth progress, and their yields. Also be sure to note any techniques you used and dates!

Keep It Clean!

It may be one of the last things on your mind as your season comes to an end but remember to give a little love to your garden tools. Take some time to clean them before you put them away for the winter. They'll last longer and be ready to use next spring!

PAINTED GARDEN TOOLS

Never lose your garden tools again! Paint the handles a bright color before using them this spring!

X Marks The Spot

Specific plants require different types of care so it is important to keep track by marking your garden. I like to get a little creative! Use old, broken terracotta planting pots or scrap wood and craft paint to create cute signs for each type of plant in your garden. They're not only pretty but they're reusable too!

"Nothing is more the child of art than a garden."

SIR WALTER SCOTT

What's the Buzz?

Did you know you could attract bees to your garden by planting certain types of flowers? Bees are attracted to blue, purple, white, and yellow flowers. Bonus points if you plant flowers with a single petal! Flowers with only one petal have more pollen and are easier for bees to crawl across.

Attracting butterflies to a garden brings color and movement. Consider planting Aster, Bee Balm, Butterfly Bushes (surprise!), Daylilies, lavender, lilac, and lupine to bring these dainty creatures to your garden!

LEARN FROM YOUR NEIGHBOR

Even if you do your research, it can be hard to pinpoint exactly how your garden will grow. Take a walk and chat with your neighbors! See what worked for them — chances are you'll both have similar results!

pH

It's important to understand the specific environment that your plants need to grow. Most state departments of agriculture typically have soil laboratories you can send samples to for pH testing or free kits to do it at home. With this information, you can either adjust the pH or choose different plants that are more suitable for your soil!

HYDRANGEAS

Hydrangeas are one of my favorite flowers and can help you better understand the science behind soil acidity! Acidic soil (pH 5 or lower) will yield blue flowers. In neutral soil (pH 5.5–6.5) hydrangeas will bloom purple. A pH higher than 6.5 will cause the flowers to become a vibrant pink.

"All gardening is landscape painting."

ALEXANDER POPE

Feed Your Garden

When you use organic matter such as manure and humus, your plants have an easier time absorbing nutrients. This means your plants will be able to live in a wider pH range!

PERENNIALS

Looking to make an investment once and see its effects for years to come? Consider growing perennials! Some of my favorites are strawberries, raspberries, blueberries, and rhubarb. If you're growing flowers, try irises, coneflowers, balloon flowers, tulips, daffodils, lilies, and Russian sage.

Handle With Care

When you first put seedlings in your garden they are very vulnerable. They need to be slowly introduced to sunlight, so keep them partially shaded. I recommend using a shade cloth, which can be placed lightly on top of your plants after they get several hours of sunlight!

"Just living is not enough...one must have sunshine, freedom, and a little flower."

HANS CHRISTIAN ANDERSEN

Save the Seeds!

If you loved the particular blooms on a flower, or found the fruits on a bush to be especially sweet, take a bit of time to retrieve their seeds. Once they're harvested and cleaned, store in marked bags with their name and date. Plant next year and enjoy them all over again!

Easiest (and tastiest) Herbs To Grow

If you're new to gardening but want fresh herbs to use in a variety of dishes, try some of these easy-to-grow herbs:

- Basil
- Cilantro
- Mint
(keep in a pot—it grows like crazy!)
- Parsley
- Rosemary
- Thyme

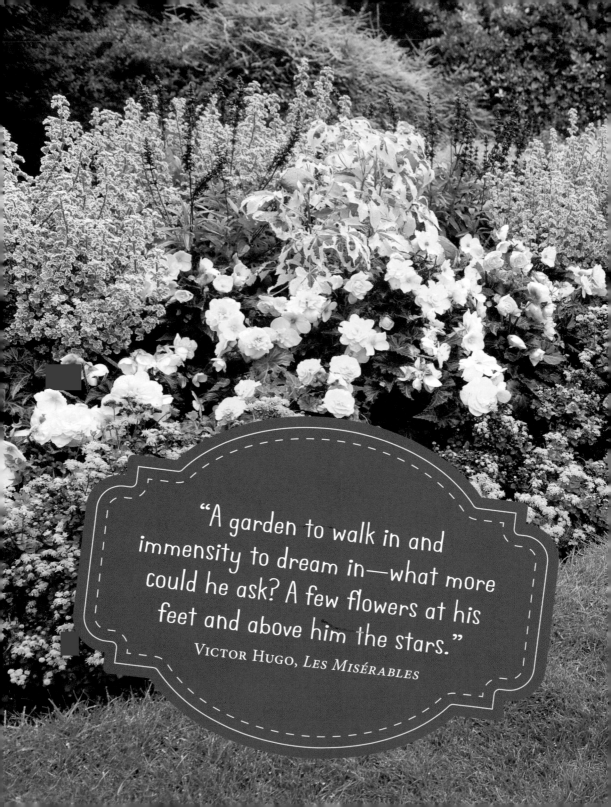

"A garden to walk in and immensity to dream in—what more could he ask? A few flowers at his feet and above him the stars."

VICTOR HUGO, LES MISÉRABLES

ROSEMARY RENEWAL

Rosemary is easy to propagate: just cut a few sprigs and stick them in soil. In no time the sprigs should root!

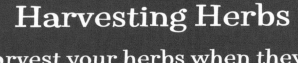

Harvesting Herbs

Harvest your herbs when they're about to flower. They'll have lots of natural oils, which add to the flavors and aromas!

HOW TO STORE HERBS

Storing herbs not only extends their lives, but it also maintains their freshness! Try oven drying, hang drying, or freezing (anything but microwave drying)! With high-moisture herbs like mint, tarragon, and basil, it's best to oven dry them since the moisture from hang drying promotes mold. Low-moisture herbs like thyme, rosemary, and dill are much more suited for hang drying!

OVEN DRYING HERBS

1. Preheat oven to *lowest* possible setting.

2. Clean herbs and pick off any dried leaves.

3. Lay herbs flat on a roasting pan.

4. Once oven is ready, pop them in for no more that 5-7 minutes. *Keep an eye on them!* Depending on the amount of moisture, your herbs can burn if you don't pay attention!

HANG DRYING HERBS

1. Pinch off any dried leaves and pat dry (removing any dew left on leaves).

2. Use twine, string, or even dental floss to tie stems together in bunches of about 12 with long stems.

3. Optional: To prevent your herbs from collecting dust, cover herbs with a small paper bag. Cut holes in the bag to provide airflow.

4. Hang in a dark place with good ventilation. The sun can cause herbs to lose their aroma. Be sure they have air so that mold doesn't grow on their leaves.

5. After 2-4 weeks they should be fully dry and ready to store.

So I Dried My Herbs...
Now What?

Dried herbs are best stored in
airtight containers like glass jars
or tightly sealed plastic bags.
Herbs that are properly dried
and stored should last
about a year!

Freezing Herbs

Keep your herbs fresh for an extra-long period of time by freezing them! Chop or blend them and store them in either olive oil or canola oil. Place the mixture in a plastic bag, flatten, and throw in the freezer! *Voila*—frozen herbs!

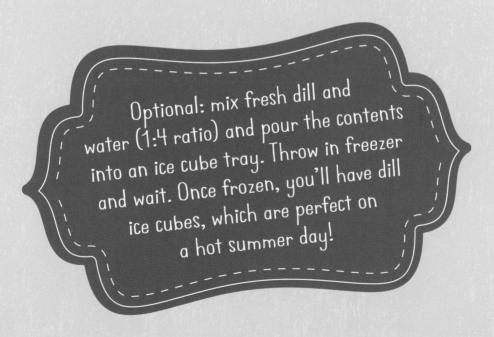

Optional: mix fresh dill and water (1:4 ratio) and pour the contents into an ice cube tray. Throw in freezer and wait. Once frozen, you'll have dill ice cubes, which are perfect on a hot summer day!

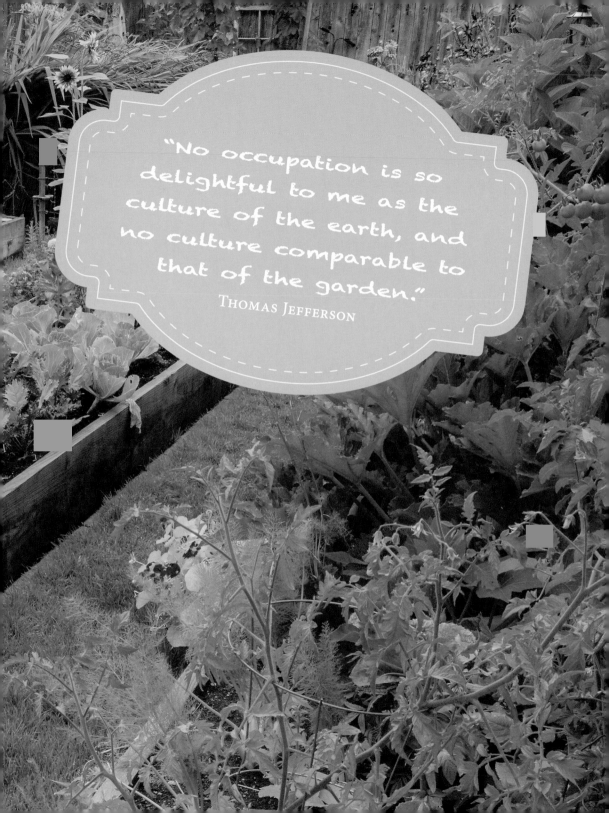

"No occupation is so delightful to me as the culture of the earth, and no culture comparable to that of the garden."

THOMAS JEFFERSON

Mint Tea

One of the most calming and refreshing drinks all-year-round is mint tea. Dry your mint, and then let 2-4 leaves steep for five minutes or so in a mug of water! Serve with honey for a sweet touch!

ELEGANT ICE

Looking for a charming way to impress guests? Freeze edible flowers into ice cubes and serve in drinks and soups! Try: rose petals, geranium petals, marigolds, violets, small pansies, herbs, and herb flowers.

Mosquitos Be Gone!

Mosquitos know how to ruin any nice night in the backyard. Fight back by planting lemon grass, catnip, marigold, and lemon thyme!

Perfumed Potpourri

You'll need dried flowers, herbs, essential oils, an airtight container, and a decorative bowl. Let your ingredients (my favorites are mint, vanilla beans, lemon peel, apple peels, lavender, cinnamon, and thyme) sit for two weeks in an airtight container, and then transfer to a decorative bowl. Enjoy!

Note: The longer you let your flowers or herbs sit, the stronger the scent!

Antipasto Platter

Looking for the perfect additions to your antipasto platter? Forget the grocery store produce; use your garden! Try using roasted asparagus, raw snap peas, spring onions or scallions, tomatoes, pickles, and peppers. Combine with prosciutto, salami, various cheeses, and olives for a colorful and delicious appetizer.

"The glory of gardening: hands in the dirt, head in the sun, heart with nature. To nurture a garden is to feed not just the body, but the soul."

ALFRED AUSTIN

Crispy Kale Chips

Kale chips are one of the easiest, most satisfying snacks you can have on hand. If you use kale from your garden, these chips barely cost anything!

Ingredients:
Kale (one bunch)
1 tablespoon extra-virgin olive oil
2 garlic cloves, minced
Sea salt

Directions
1. Preheat oven to 350°F
2. Remove the stems of the kale. Rip into smaller, "chip-sized" pieces. Wash and dry thoroughly.
3. Combine kale, salt, ½ tablespoon olive oil, and garlic into a mixing bowl.
4. Lightly line two baking trays with the remaining ½ tablespoon of olive oil and lay kale out flat without overlapping too much.
5. Bake for 12-15 minutes until crisp.

Garden Fresh Bruschetta

This fresh appetizer is sure to be a hit, especially if you use the tomatoes from your garden!

Yield: 20 pieces

Ingredients:
¼ cup extra-virgin olive oil
3 tablespoons basil, finely chopped
4 garlic cloves, minced
Sea salt
Coarsely ground black pepper
4 medium tomatoes, diced
3 tablespoons grated Parmesan cheese
1 baguette, charred

Optional:
Mozzarella cheese

Directions:
1. Toss tomatoes with oil, basil, garlic, salt, and pepper. Sprinkle on the Parmesan and refrigerate for a minimum of 1 hour.
2. Cut bread into thin slices and toast in oven until lightly browned. Top with tomato mixture (best if brought back to room temperature). Add mozzarella if desired. Serve immediately because the bread will get soggy.

Brown Sugar Butternut Squash

This simple recipe brings butternut squash's sweetness to the next level! Not to mention you only need three ingredients!

Ingredients:
2 squash, peeled and cubed
2 tablespoons brown sugar
3 tablespoons unsalted butter

Optional
2 sprigs, thyme
4 bay leaves

Directions:
1. Preheat your oven to 400°F.
2. Place squash on a parchment paper lined baking tray. Melt butter and pour over the squash. Sprinkle the brown sugar on top. Toss carefully.
3. Roast for 40 minutes until caramelized.
4. Remove from oven and serve immediately. Optional: Garnish with thyme and bay leaves.

Cranberry Zucchini Muffins

Those who have grown zucchini know that you're often left with quite a few extra. Put them to good use with these delicious zucchini muffins.

Yields: 14 Muffins

Ingredients:
3 cups zucchini, grated
⅔ cup unsalted butter, melted
1 ⅓ cup sugar
2 eggs, beaten
2 teaspoons vanilla
2 teaspoons baking soda
Sea salt
3 cups all-purpose flour
2 teaspoons cinnamon
½ teaspoon nutmeg
1 cup dried cranberries

Directions:
1. Preheat the oven to 350°F.
2. Combine the sugar, eggs, and vanilla in a large bowl and mix in the grated zucchini. Once stirred in, add the melted butter.
3. Mix together the flour, baking soda, nutmeg, cinnamon, and salt in a separate bowl. Add the dry ingredients into the zucchini mixture, followed by the cranberries.
4. Use muffin tins or coat the muffin tray with non-stick cooking spray. Spoon the mixture into the tray filling each cup up completely.
5. Bake on the middle rack for 20 to 25 minutes until muffins are golden brown. Test with a long toothpick to ensure the muffins have cooked all the way through.
6. Leave out to cool on a cooling rack for 15 minutes and enjoy!

ON
PRESERVING &
CANNING

"A GOOD GARDEN MAY HAVE SOME WEEDS."

Thomas Fuller

Mind the Gap!

Headspace is the gap between
the product you're canning and
the rim of the jar. It usually
ranges from ½ to ¼ inch and
should be included in your recipe.
As the contents of your
jar are heated, they expand.
If they reach the rim of the jar
they will prevent your jar
from sealing properly.

What can I reuse?

Canning doesn't have to be an expensive process! You can actually reuse both the jars and the metal rings, but never reuse the lids. Once they're used the first time, seals will not properly form again. Lids are sold in packs wherever you buy your canning materials.

PRESSURE CANNING VERSUS WATER BATH?

The canning method you choose depends on the acidity of the product you are looking to process. Higher-acid foods like fruits, berries, and some vegetables are best canned using the water bath method. Lower-acid foods, however, *must* be canned using the pressure canning method.

Pressure Canning Trick

Make your life easier by greasing the lid of your pressure canner before using it! Use petroleum jelly to ensure that the top comes off, allowing you easy access to your freshly canned goods.

WATER BATH CANNING: TOWEL TRICK

Your jars should never touch the bottom of the canner or pot you are using for your water bath. There are baskets and trays you can buy to insert into the pot to ensure this doesn't happen or you can just use an old dishtowel. The towel is much less expensive and fits into any size pot!

"What is a weed? A plant whose virtues have never been discovered."

RALPH WALDO EMERSON

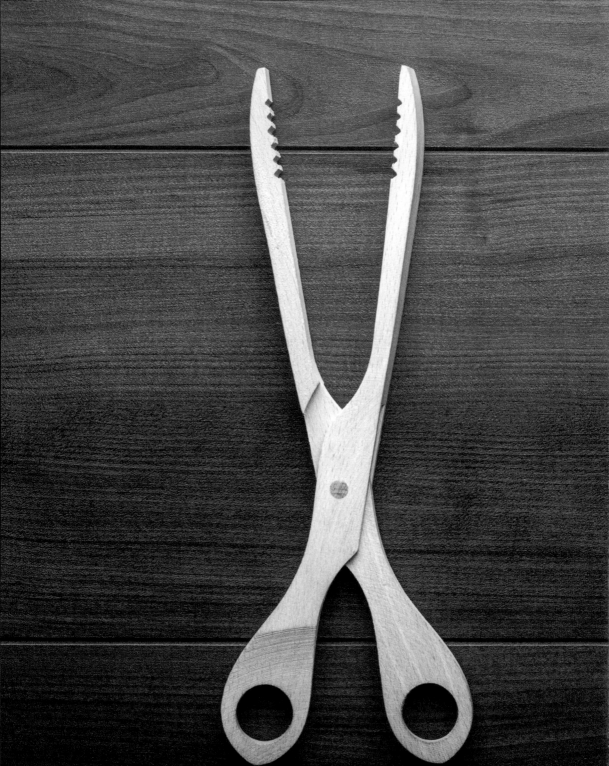

WATER BATH CANNING:
TOOLS

Two canning essentials are grabbers and a funnel. The funnel will ensure that no excess jam or jelly lands on the rim where the vacuum seal will be created. The grabbers protect your skin from being burned by the hot jars and boiling water. Plus, once your jars are in the water bath it's nearly impossible to get them out without grabbers.

Don't Cut Corners

Canning comes down to science,
and cutting corners can result in
a tainted final product. Once
you've poured your product into
your jar make sure you take a
spatula or plastic knife and run
it around the inside walls of your
jar, releasing air bubbles trapped
inside. Also, be sure to wipe
the rim of the jar with a wet cloth
before putting the top on.

WHY WARM JARS?

Warming your jars before pouring food into them not only further sanitizes your jar after cleaning it, but it also prevents the jar from cracking with the heat!

Water Bath Canning: Elevation

Did you know that elevation affects canning? The higher your altitude, the longer your boil time. There are many resources online to help you to choose the best amount of time based on your location!

QUALITY IS EVERYTHING!

Remember that what you start with is what you end up with. No matter how strong the pickling or processing, your outcome goes hand-in-hand with the quality of the ingredients you utilize. Make sure that you know the full story to your ingredients: i.e. use vegetables only grown in your own garden!

"IF I HAD A FLOWER FOR EVERY TIME I THOUGHT OF YOU...I COULD WALK THROUGH MY GARDEN FOREVER."

ALFRED TENNYSON

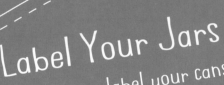

Label Your Jars

Always, always, always label your cans! Jot down the name and date of processing on each jar so that you won't have to guess whether or not the canned foods are still good later in the year!

GIFT YOUR CANNED FOODS!

Your homemade jams, preserves, and sauces can make amazing (and beautiful) gifts! Wrap twine and a gift tag around your glass jar and *voila*, you've created an inexpensive yet thoughtful gift for just about anyone!

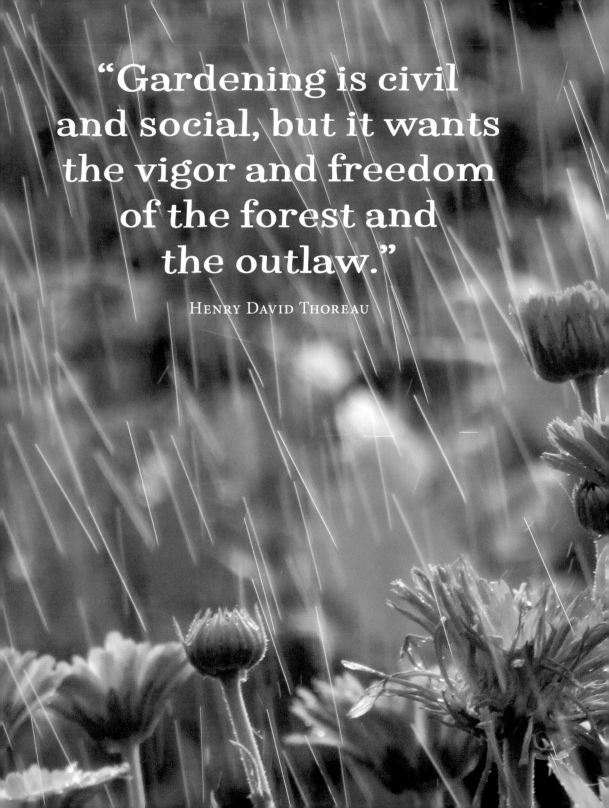

"Gardening is civil
and social, but it wants
the vigor and freedom
of the forest and
the outlaw."

Henry David Thoreau

Applesauce

The fall often leaves you with an abundance of apples, sometimes far too many to eat before they go bad. Don't let them go to waste! Put them to good use and enjoy them throughout the year!

Yields: 15 pints

Ingredients:
4 pounds apples
½ cup apple cider or water

Optional:
1 tablespoon cinnamon
1 teaspoon grated nutmeg
½ teaspoon cloves
Pinch of sugar

Directions

1. Clean jars and preheat them by placing them into a canner and bringing the water to a simmer, *not a boil*. Make sure you have a rack, basket, or towel in the bottom of your canner. Heat lids as well, keeping them heated until you are ready to use.
2. After removing the cores, cut apples into quarters, and then place in large pot and add apple cider or water. Put the lid on the pot and let simmer for 15-20 minutes until it has broken down. Remove apple skins with tongs, and use a potato masher to further break down fruit. Optional: add additional spices to taste.
3. Using jar grabbers, remove one jar at a time from the canner. Place canning funnel into jar and ladle applesauce into the jar leaving ½-inch headspace. Take a spatula or plastic knife and run along the side of the jar to remove any air bubbles. Wipe the rim with a wet cloth to remove any excess sauce and use tongs to place a hot lid on the jar. Gently screw on the band and place jars back in canner.
4. Once all of the jars are in the canner, make sure that each jar is covered by at least an inch of water. Cover the canner with a lid and bring to a rolling boil for 15 minutes. Remove jars and let them rest for 24 hours.
5. Once cooled, check that the jars have sealed properly by pressing on the top. If they "click" they're not sealed and should be reprocessed or refrigerated and eaten within the next two weeks. If the lid shows no movement, store in a dark cool place and enjoy for up to a year later!

Raspberry Jam

Raspberry jam is excellent with toast and coffee, and one of my favorite ways to eat raspberry jam is on ham sandwiches... it may sound odd, but think of it like cranberry sauce and turkey!

Yields: 9 cups

Ingredients:
5 cups red or black raspberries
7 cups granulated sugar
1 ¾ ounces pectin
½ teaspoon butter

Directions
1. Clean jars and preheat them by placing them into a canner and bringing the water to a simmer, *not a boil*. Make sure you have a rack, basket, or towel in the bottom of your canner. Heat lids as well, keeping them heated until you are ready to use.
2. Lightly crush raspberries—*don't puree*—one cup at a time. If desired, sieve half of the raspberries to remove seeds.
3. Combine raspberries, pectin, and butter into a saucepan on medium-high heat. Stir constantly until the mixture is brought to a full boil. Add the sugar and continue boiling, stirring constantly, for one minute. Remove from heat and skim off foam.
4. Using jar grabbers, remove one jar at a time from the canner. Place canning funnel into jar and ladle applesauce into the jar leaving ½-inch headspace. Take a spatula or plastic knife and run along the side of the jar to remove any air bubbles. Wipe the rim with a wet cloth to remove any excess sauce and use tongs to place a hot lid on the jar. Gently screw on the band and place jars back in canner.
5. Once all of the jars are in the canner, make sure that each jar is covered by at least an inch of water. Cover the canner with a lid and bring to a rolling boil for 10 minutes. Turn off the burner, and let the jars process for another 5 minutes. Remove the jars and let cool for 24 hours.
6. Once cooled, check that the jars have sealed properly by pressing on the top. If they "click" they're not sealed and should be reprocessed or refrigerated and eaten within the next two weeks. If the lid shows no movement, store in a dark cool place and enjoy for up to a year later!

Blueberry Jam

Blueberry jam is a well-loved classic when it comes to canning. This recipe is perfect if you're new to canning! Give it a try—I'm sure you'll love the result!

Yields: 4 pints

Ingredients:
4 ½ cups of blueberries (crushed)
4 Tablespoons of lemon juice
7 cups of granulated sugar
6 ounces of liquid pectin

Directions:
1. Clean jars and preheat them by placing them into a canner and bringing the water to a simmer, *not a boil*. Make sure you have a rack, basket, or towel in the bottom of your canner. Heat lids as well, keeping them heated until you are ready to use.
2. Combine blueberries, lemon juice, and sugar into a saucepan on high heat. Stir constantly until the mixture is brought to a full boil. Stirring constantly, add in the pectin and cook for one minute. Remove from heat and skim off foam.
3. Using jar grabbers, remove one jar at a time from the canner. Place canning funnel into jar and ladle applesauce into the jar leaving ½-inch headspace. Take a spatula or plastic knife and run along the side of the jar to remove any air bubbles. Wipe the rim with a wet cloth to remove any excess sauce and use tongs to place a hot lid on the jar. Gently screw on the band and place jars back in canner.
4. Once all of the jars are in the canner, make sure that each jar is covered by at least an inch of water. Cover the canner with a lid and bring to a rolling boil for 10 minutes. Turn off the burner, and let the jars process for another 5 minutes. Remove the jars and let cool for 24 hours.
5. Once cooled, check that the jars have sealed properly by pressing on the top. If they "click" they're not sealed and should be reprocessed or refrigerated and eaten within the next two weeks. If the lid shows no movement, store in a dark cool place and enjoy for up to a year later!

Green Beans (or Carrots!)

Enjoy green beans from your garden all year round using this pressure canning recipe, which can also double for carrots!

1. Clean jars and preheat them by placing them into a canner and bringing the water to a simmer, *not a boil*. Make sure you have a rack, basket, or towel in the bottom of your canner. Heat lids as well, keeping them heated until you are ready to use.
2. Using jar grabbers, remove one jar at a time from the canner and place on a heat-protected surface. Using a canning funnel, add your washed and cut green beans into a jar. Add salt to taste (usually a ½ teaspoon is enough for a pint).
3. Pour boiling water over the beans, leaving 1-inch headspace. Take a spatula or plastic knife and run along the side of the jar to remove any air bubbles. Wipe the rim with a wet cloth to remove any excess sauce and use tongs to place a hot lid on the jar. Gently screw on the band and place jars back in canner.
4. Make sure there are between 2-3 inches of water in your pressure canner. Process at 10 pounds of pressure for 20 minutes.
5. Next, carefully remove the canner's lid and place the jars on a cooling rack using grabbers. Let cool for 24 hours.
6. Finally, check that the jars have sealed properly by pressing on the top. If they "click" they're not sealed and should be reprocessed or refrigerated and eaten within the next two weeks. If the lid shows no movement, store in a dark cool place and enjoy for up to a year later!

About the Author

Emily Mills grew up in a small, Connecticut town. Her home was sandwiched between two farms where her appreciation for gardening was fostered: picking raspberries as a child and bringing home fresh eggs for her mother to scramble. Emily's family spent many summer nights eating squash from her father's garden and many winter mornings cracking open jars of her cousin's unparalleled blueberry jam. Throughout the years, she has picked up quite a few tips and tricks that she hopes can be of use to you in your garden!

About Cider Mill Press Book Publishers

Good ideas ripen with time. From seed to harvest, Cider Mill Press
brings fine reading, information, and entertainment together between
the covers of its creatively crafted books. Our Cider Mill bears fruit
twice a year, publishing a new crop of titles each spring and fall.

"Where Good Books Are Ready for Press"

Visit us on the Web at
www.cidermillpress.com
or write to us at
PO Box 454
12 Spring St.
Kennebunkport, Maine 04046